North Carolina LGBT Legal Guide

The Landscape of Legal Equality

Lorin G. Page, Esq.

North Carolina LGBT Legal Guide

Printed by:
CreateSpace Independent Publishing Platform

Copyright © 2017, Lorin G. Page, Esq.

Published in the United States of America

Book ID: 170302-00716-2

ISBN-13: 978-1975893439
ISBN-10: 1975893433

No parts of this publication may be reproduced without correct attribution to the author of this book.

For more information on 90-Minute Books including how you can publish your own book, visit www.90minutebooks.com or call (863) 318-0464

Disclaimer: This Guide is just that, a guide, and is intended for informational purposes only. It is not a substitute for professional advice on any of the topics discussed, and it should not be relied upon by anyone as a basis for taking any actions. Neither is it a work of scholarship, and does not purport to follow the standard conventions for citation of sources

Here's What's Inside...

A Note From The Author 1

Introduction 2

Chapter 1: Welcome To Marriage 8

Chapter 2: Marriage and Money 24

Chapter 3: Action Items 48

Conclusion 58

About the Author 60

A Note From The Author

I wrote this manual for a simple reason – I believe in legal equality for the LGBT community.

As with other civil rights movements, the battle for equal rights for the LGBT community requires a collective, active and informed effort to advance, but these advancements are meaningless if the rights they secure are not understood and exercised.

I hope this guide helps members of the LGBT community in North Carolina fully enjoy the equal rights they now possess.

If you have any questions, please feel free to contact me at 1-828-696-1811 or lorin@strausslaw.com.

Thank You,

Lorin

Introduction

On June 26, 2015, the Supreme Court issued one of the most sweeping civil rights decisions in its history. By granting full legal equality to marriages between consenting, homosexual adults, <u>Obergefell v. Hodges</u> elevated millions of Americans from second class to full citizens. It is hard to overestimate the symbolic significance of this ruling for the LGBT community and their allies, but suffice it to say that the word "Obergefell" has become nearly synonymous with legal equality for LGBT individuals. It has become, for many Americans, a symbol of hope, acceptance and a faith in democratic institutions.

But, of course, <u>Obergefell</u> is more than simply a symbol, and legal equality is about more than simply acceptance. In our society, marriage confers a panoply of legal rights. Married couples have preferential tax treatment in many ways, from income to estate tax. The law often establishes presumptive spousal rights involving inheritance or IRA beneficiary designation and creates legal presumptions in favor of spouses serving as Guardian and making health care decisions. In some states, adopting as a married step-parent is much easier than adopting as an unmarried step-parent.

And, of course, with marriage comes divorce – as gay couples are now enjoying the economic benefits of legal equality, they also face the unpleasantness of unwinding a marriage.

Why a Legal Guide?

Considering the sweeping breadth of <u>Obergefell</u>, one might sensibly summarize the current status of LGBT rights as "legal equality," and that's true. So why the need for a LGBT legal guide?

First, education: a whole community of people are now learning exactly what legal "equality" means. Before <u>Obergefell</u>, the legal intricacies and benefits of marriage were simply irrelevant to many LGBT individuals, and so they may be unfamiliar. Legal rights must be understood to be exercised.

Second, while <u>Obergefell</u> established legal equality in broad terms, many details of what that means will need to be fleshed out in lower courts. The battle is not over, and educating the LGBT and ally community about LGBT legal helps ensure continued progress.

Third, because despite legal gains, discrimination against LGBT individuals is still widespread, and publishing a guide helps to give LGBT individuals a better understanding of what are their legal rights, who are their allies and how to mainstream acceptance of legal equality among non LGBT individuals.

Fourth and finally, because in addition to enjoying new rights, there are still a few possibilities for remedial action by which LGBT individuals can use <u>Obergefell</u> to help unwind previous injustice – filing an amended income or estate tax return, for instance, or appealing a previous denial of survivorship benefits. By doing so, LGBT individuals and couples might be able to take actions that will improve their finances.

What's in this Legal Guide?

From a legal perspective, marriage is a civil institution governed under state law. While <u>Obergefell</u> was decided by the Supreme Court of the Unites States, a branch of the federal government, the clear majority of the laws that affect marital rights are found in state statutes, and even those federal laws that deal with marriage turn upon whether an individual is married under a given state's laws. The first section of this guide considers the state law parameters of marriage, in particular the body of legal rights and obligations commonly called family or domestic law. Next, we consider the financial implications of marriage, including topics like income and estate tax reporting, IRA beneficiary designations and probate. Finally, in the third section, we focus on practical considerations and possible remedial actions for LGBT individuals or couples.

A Short Note about the History of LGBT Rights in America

"Gay Marriage," as legal marriage equality for LGBT individuals is often described, has been a long time coming. While a history of numerous and noxious laws criminalizing and otherwise marginalizing LGBT individuals is beyond the scope of this Guide, it is helpful as a point of reference to recall that as recently as 2003 a divided Supreme Court of the United States found itself, in Lawrence v. Texas, striking down states law that criminalized homosexual behavior.

Since then, over the last fifteen years, LGBT rights activists have won numerous battles in state and federal courts, dramatically turning the tide on LGBT rights in America in a . Lawrence was a 5-4 decision, overturning a prior 5-4 decision in the 1986 SCOTUS case of Bowers v. Hardwick, which upheld a statute criminalizing homosexual contact. At the time of Lawrence, 38 states still had statutory or constitutional prohibitions on gay marriage. By 2014, the country was split in half between states allowing gay marriage and those prohibiting it – many of which had since 2000 incorporated special prohibitions on gay marriage into their state constitutions. [1]

North Carolina is one such state. On May 8, 2012, voters passed a constitutional amendment outlawing gay marriage. For the next two years, legal challenges worked their way through courts. In the 2014 case of <u>General Synod of the United Church of Christ v. Cooper</u>, Judge Cogburn of the United States District Court for the Western District of North Carolina ruled that the State's laws denying marriage rights to same-sex couples married elsewhere and criminalizing the solemnization of same-sex marriages were unconstitutional. Judge Cogburn concluded that "it clear as a matter of what is now settled law in the Fourth Circuit that North Carolina laws prohibiting same-sex marriage, refusing to recognize same-sex marriages originating elsewhere, and/or threatening to penalize those who would solemnize such marriages, are unconstitutional."[2] After the Fourth Circuit Court of Appeals upheld a ruling in <u>Bostic v. Schaefer</u> that struck down a Virginia same-sex marriage ban, Roy Cooper, then acting Attorney General of North Carolina, declined to appeal.

Thus, even before <u>Obergefell</u>, same-sex marriage has been legally recognized in NC since October 10, 2014. Yet while the <u>General Synod</u> and

---

[1] www.graphics.latimes.com/usmap-gay-marriage-chronology
[2] <u>General Synod of the United Church of Christ v. Cooper</u>

Bostic cases advanced LGBT rights in North Carolina, those rulings were both narrower and less enduring than the Supreme Court's ruling in Obergefell.

In Obergefell v. Hodges, the Supreme Court faced a constitutional dilemma impacting millions of Americans reduced into two legal questions:

1) Does the Fourteenth Amendment require a state to license a marriage between two people of the same sex?
2) Does the Fourteenth Amendment require a state to recognize a marriage between two people of the same sex that was legally licensed and performed in another state?

By answering both in the affirmative, the Supreme Court of the United States ushered in a new era for LBGT Americans.

Chapter 1: Welcome To Marriage

What is Marriage?

As a legal institution, marriage is an agreement between two adults governed by statute and memorialized by registration with the state which confers several benefits and obligations.

In North Carolina, to marry, two adults need only go to the courthouse, file paperwork, and pay a fee. The statutory requirements to marry under the laws of North Carolina require two people to: obtain a marriage license; have a ceremony conducted by an authorized person in which both parties are present and consent to marriage; not be too closely related or married to someone else; and be 18 or older without parental consent, 16-17 years old with parental consent, or may even be 14-15 years old with court approval under limited circumstances.[3]

Domestic Partnerships, Civil Unions and Common Law Marriage

What isn't marriage? Anything other than a legal marriage as described above or validly performed in another jurisdiction. In the years before Obergefell, as various state courts and legislatures figured out how to approach the

---

[3] N.C.G.S. § § 51-1

question of gay marriage, several novel legal categories were developed.

Two such legal categories are a "Domestic Partnerships" and "Civil Unions," marriage alternatives that were created by certain states to give LGBT couples certain rights traditionally available only to same-sex couples. Domestic partnerships and Civil Unions are non-marital relationships between two legal adults who live together as couple. Generally speaking, they were created as an equivalent to marriage for the purpose of conferring employee-partner benefits otherwise reserved for spouses. While neither Domestic partnerships nor Civil Unions are recognized under North Carolina law, businesses and municipal governments are permitted to offer benefits to domestic partners and several have opted to do so. In those municipalities, in order to claim spousal benefits an individual must file a domestic partnership certificate.

For purposes of Federal taxation, the Internal Revenue Service does not recognize civil unions or domestic partnerships,[4] and the extent to which state courts recognize them varies widely. In New Jersey, for instance, the state's Tax Court did not allow a same sex domestic partner to get a spousal estate tax deduction as a surviving spouse because the couple was neither married

---

[4] www.irs.gov/irb/2015-45_IRB/ar09.html

nor in a civil union under New Jersey's Domestic Partnership Act (DPA), and therefore did not qualify to be treated as a spouse for estate tax purposes.[5] The Social Security Administration, in contrast, does consider civil unions and domestic partnerships as equivalent to marriage in certain circumstances.

Finally, another version of marriage is "common law marriage," a judicial doctrine in certain states that considers two people to be married if they have lived together for a period of years. Though repealed by statute in most states, in those states in which the common law marriages are still recognized, it confers the same legal benefits as statutory marriages.

Common law marriage no longer exists in North Carolina, but a valid common law marriage from another state will be recognized. It is unclear, however, how <u>Obergefell</u> will affect common law marriages, or rather, claims by LGBT couples that they were, in fact married, in those states. Because <u>Obergefell</u> struck down discriminatory laws on marriage as unconstitutional, but did not specifically address the question of retroactive application, these issues will have to be litigated. Courts may apply the ruling retroactively in ways that would open up a cauldron of litigation.

---

[5] www.bna.com/samesex-partner-not-n57982072523

Family Law Aspects of Marriage

Marriage confers a whole suite of rights and obligations upon spouses under both state and federal law. In addition to the financial benefits discussed in the next chapter, spousal rights crop up in a variety of other legal arenas: real property, inheritance, contract, bankruptcy, criminal, and, obviously family law. The preponderance of the rights and obligations that accompany marriage and associated relationships under the laws of the various states are often called "family law." This body of law governs relationships between married persons and their children: marriage, divorce and equitable distribution, adoption, child custody, support.

The full scope of these rights is far beyond this guide, but the pages that follow address some core ones before turning to the finances.

Premarital Agreements

For couples who use pre-marital or pre-nuptial contracts, they are the first part of the legal relationship by which parties agree to treat their respective property as separate during the marriage and in the event of divorce, waiving the statutory property rights that normally accompany marriage and divorce.

North Carolina General Statute Chapter 52B, the "Uniform Premarital Agreement Act," provides that parties to a premarital can agree in advance to resolve a potential future division of real and personal property, alimony or child custody or support (as long as the arrangement is in best interests of child at time divorce, it will be upheld). The law does not uphold child custody or support arrangements that do not meet the needs of the child.

In North Carolina, a valid a premarital contract must be in writing, voluntarily negotiated, signed by both parties, and must meet a few other requirements. The agreement cannot be "unconscionable," or too unfair to one party. An agreement is unconscionable if, when it was executed, one party "was not provided a fair and reasonable disclosure of the property or financial obligations of the other party; did not voluntarily and expressly waive, in writing, any right to disclosure of the property or financial obligations of the other party beyond the disclosure provided, and did not have, or reasonably could not have had, an adequate knowledge of the property or financial obligations of the other party."[6]

---

[6] N.C.G.S. § 52B-7(a)(2)

Divorce

If there is no pre-marital contract, the process of divorce is more involved. Divorce in North Carolina is governed by Chapter 50 of the General Statutes. The majority of divorces are uncontested and parties proceed under N.C.G.S § 50-6, which provides that "marriages may be dissolved and the parties thereto divorced from the bonds of matrimony on the application of either party, if and when the husband and wife have lived separate and apart for one year, and the plaintiff or defendant in the suit for divorce has resided in the State for a period of six months."

This is called an "Absolute Divorce" and is the traditional "no-fault" divorce. The parties must have been separated for one-year, living separate and apart with no intent on the part of either spouse to resume the marital relationship. If the parties reconcile during that one year period, the clock starts all over again, with the exception that "isolated incidents of sexual intercourse between the parties shall not toll the statutory period required for divorce predicated on separation of one year."[7]

Crucial to note for those contemplating divorce is that actions for spousal support and equitable distribution must be initiated at time of divorce

---

[7] N.C.G.S. § 50-6

and cannot be raised after divorce is granted. Moreover, while custody of a minor child always remains within the jurisdiction of a court, this should also be raised and resolved in during divorce to avoid prolonged conflicts.

The effects of absolute divorce are set forth in N.C.G.S § 50-11. The first and most obvious of consequences is that "all rights arising out of the marriage shall cease and determine except as hereinafter set out, and either party may marry again without restriction arising from the dissolved marriage."[8]

Unless it specifically deals with other postseparation rights, however, a divorce decree does not, by itself, resolve financial questions. In order for a judgement of divorce to "affect the rights of either spouse with respect to any action for alimony or postseparation support pending at the time the judgment for divorce is granted" or to "impair or destroy the right of a spouse to receive alimony or postseparation support or affect any other rights provided for such spouse under any judgment or decree of a court rendered before or at the time of the judgment of absolute divorce" It must be accompanied by a request for equitable distribution. [9] It is imperative that parties to a divorce assert claims to equitable distribution *before* the final decree

---

[8] N.C.G.S. § 50-11(a)
[9] *Id.*

of divorce, as, with limited exceptions, absolute divorce "shall destroy the right of a spouse to equitable distribution under G.S. 50-20 unless the right is asserted prior to judgment of absolute divorce."[10]

How to Divorce

The process of securing an uncontested divorce is comparatively simple. First of all, most uncontested divorces proceed according to a "separation agreement," or "consent agreement," a contract entered into between spouses in anticipation of an uncontested divorce that address issues such as property division, custody, and spousal support from time of separation forward. Separation agreements are voluntary contracts entered into by the two parties and are not required as a part of absolute divorce.

A valid separation agreement must be in writing and signed by both parties before a certifying officer such as a notary. A court will not enforce provisions of a separation agreement if the agreement is unconscionable in light of all circumstances or was obtained under duress.

Unless a separation agreement is submitted to the court and endorsed by a judge, it is enforceable only as a contract. However, if

---

[10] *Id.*

submitted to the court, the agreement becomes part of the court record, meaning it can be modified only with judicial consent and that violation of its terms subjects the offending party to contempt of court. As always, any child custody or support provisions of a separation agreement are enforceable only to the extent they are in the best interests of the minor child.

To begin the court process of divorce, an individual must complete and file a Complaint for Absolute Divorce with the Clerk of Court in the county in which they live, along with a Domestic Civil Action Cover Sheet and a Civil Summons. After filing the forms, a copy must be served on the other spouse by the Sheriff's Department in your county.

The spouse seeking divorce must then wait thirty days to allow an opportunity to respond, after which they must schedule a hearing before the Clerk of Court. A Notice of Hearing form is brought to the Clerk of Court, whose office schedules a date and time for the hearing. The Notice of Hearing must then be served on the other spouse at least 10 days before the hearing date by First Class U.S. Mail or the Sheriff's Department.

Last, they will show up on the date of the hearing with two copies of a Judgment of Absolute

Divorce and a Certificate of Absolute Divorce, which the judge will sign, finalizing the divorce.

Contested Divorce and Divorce from Bed and Board

In the event that one spouse cannot or will not consent to divorce or sign a separation agreement, the other spouse may attempt to pursue a "Divorce from Bed and Board." While N.C.G.S §50-7 uses the anachronistic term "Divorce from Bed and Board," it is in fact not a divorce at all but a court-ordered separation that begins the period of legal separation required for Absolute Divorce, but which, unlike "absolute divorce," is fault based and.

Divorce from Bed and Board is available to an offended party whose spouse "abandons his or her family," "maliciously turns the other out of doors," "by cruel or barbarous treatment endangers the life of the other," "offers such indignities to the person of the other as to render his or her condition intolerable and life burdensome," "becomes an excessive user of alcohol or drugs so as to render the condition of the other spouse intolerable and the life of that spouse burdensome," or "commits adultery." [11]

The precise ramifications of a Divorce from Bed and Board vary from case to case, but an order

---

[11] N.C.G.S. §50-7

may significantly affect the rights of the defendant spouse. First, it helps establish a foundation for absolute divorce. But even a court does not sever the marital relationship, a decree of divorce from bed and board may affect a spouses' rights involving: alimony; postseparation support; child custody; child support; property rights in equitable distribution; cohabitation; spousal intestate succession rights; homestead rights; elective share rights; estate administration rights; or the statutory right to a year's allowance after death..[12]

Divorce and The Dollar: Equitable Distribution and Spousal Support

In North Carolina, the process of dividing a marital estate is called "equitable distribution." As part of the divorce proceedings, one or both parties will request that the court determine how much property belongs to the marital estate and how it should be divided. The spouse filing for divorce should file a separate request for equitable distribution supported by an affidavit that describes the property subject to the claim. The court will identify the property and debts of the spouses, classify that property as marital, separate or divisible, determine the net market value of the property, and divide it between the parties.

---

[12] N.C.G.S. §50

The court's goal is to make a division as close to equal as possible, but it may deviate from a numerically even division if circumstances dictate, including factors such as the length of marriage, health of parties, contributions to marriage, custodial needs, and tax consequences. For purposes of equitable distribution, adultery by one party is not a factor except when marital property was involved in the infidelity.[13]

A key question in equitable distribution cases involves determining which assets are marital and which are separate. Real and personal property acquired by either or both spouses during the marriage and before the date of separation is marital property. Separate property includes all property owned by one spouse before marriage, gifts or bequests that spouse got individually, pain and suffering awards, professional and business licenses and similar assets. Separate property can become marital property if it is sufficiently commingled in the "marital estate." Finally, property received after separation and before the date of distribution is divisible property.

Another important facet of divorce proceedings is settling the question of spousal support, which falls into two categories: post-separation support and alimony.[14] Post-separation support is a

---

[13] N.C.G.S. §50-20
[14] N.C.G.S. §50-16.3A

temporary arrangement put in place after the separation but before the final divorce. The primary focus of spousal support payments is meeting the economic needs of a dependent spouse and is not dependent on marital fault. Thus, the primary requirement for post-separation support is that there be a verifiable dependent spouse and supporting spouse. The court will order the supporting spouse to provide temporary financial support to the dependent spouse until a final order of alimony, if any, is made.

Alimony is permanent support one spouse makes to the other pursuant to a court order. As with temporary support, the court considers factors such as each spouse's earning capacity, health and age, relative earning power, education level, and separate property available.

But what about the Children?

Child Custody and Support

For a divorcing couple with children, the most important (and often the most contentious) issue is child custody. In North Carolina, child custody, like equitable distribution or spousal support may be determined by a court during a divorce upon motion by one spouse.[15]

---

[15] N.C.G.S. §50-13.1

Ideally, the spouses voluntarily agree on a custody plan of their own design. If accord is not possible, a judge might order mediation, and if this too fails, a judge will hear evidence and determine the custody arrangement. In doing so, the court is concerned primarily with the "best interest of the minor child," not parental rights.

Custody arrangements range from very simple – such as sole custody by one parent – to very complex. There are a variety of custody arrangements – joint, sole, primary or secondary – the purpose of which is to determine who makes decisions for a child and where they will reside. These arrangements are always subject to court scrutiny and are modifiable if there is a substantial change of circumstances.

Whether a divorcing parent is awarded custody or not, they may be required to pay child support. As with custody, the primary factor is the child's best interest, and as with spousal support, the court will consider the incomes of both parents.

Adoption

For many LGBT couples, adoption is among the most important aspects of legal equality. LGBT individuals and couples have faced overt discrimination in adoption proceedings for years, including laws designed to prevent homosexual individuals or couples from adopting. Even in the absence of statutory prohibitions on same sex couples adopting, LGBT persons have been subject to the indignity of being deemed "unfit" by local governmental officials assessing whether a home is suitable for a child. Further, certain forms of adoption rely upon marital rights, and to the extent that gay persons could not marry, they could not access those forms of adoption.

In North Carolina, for a child to be adopted, a biological parent (or both parents) must relinquish or be judicially deprived of their parental rights.[16] This can be done through placement with an adoption agency and the execution by the biological parents of a relinquishment or by judicial decree. While fathers can consent to relinquishment before or after the child is born, mothers can only execute the consent or relinquishment after the child is born. Both fathers and mothers have seven days within which to revoke a relinquishment.

For an agency adoption, there must be a pre-placement assessment by a licensed agency, completed within twelve months of the placement, finding that the adoptive parents are suitable. While the issue has not been fully adjudicated in North Carolina courts since Obergefell to the author's knowledge, one

---

[16] N.C.G.S. §§ 48-1 through 48-38

profound impact of the Supreme Court's ruling should be that local governmental and quasi-governmental agencies that conduct adoption assessments will be prohibited from finding same sex couples unfit simply by virtue of their sexual orientation.

For a joint adoption, in which neither spouse is a biological parent of the child, same-sex married couples in North Carolina may now jointly adopt a child through independent adoption, agency adoption or as a foster by filing a joint petition to adopt.

Step-parent adoptions, in which one spouse is a biological parent and the other is not but wishes to establish parental rights, are fully legal in North Carolina for LGBT couples.

Prior to Boseman v. Jarrell, the right to adopt was denied to married same-sex couples in North Carolina where one parent was the legal parent of the child. In 2013, a federal judge ruled in favor of Julia Boseman, the first openly gay member of the State legislature, holding that second-parent adoption is legal for same-sex couples. Challenges to the case were dropped in the wake of subsequent victories like Windsor and Obergefell, meaning that the ruling stands as law in North Carolina.

Chapter 2: Marriage and Money

While the family law rights discussed above are the most important legal aspect of marriage for most people, there are myriad financial implications as well. Marital status affects everything from taxes to pension benefits, and LGBT couples have been profoundly financially disadvantaged by their inability to legally marry. <u>Obergefell</u> grants LGBT access to the financial benefits of marriage.

Taxes

For most people, the biggest financial incentive to marrying is the preferential tax treatment that married couples enjoy. Married couples have the option to file their income taxes jointly, which may lower their combined taxable income, and an individual can also give unlimited assets to a spouse during life or at death without incurring gift or estate taxes. For many LGBT couples considering marriage for the first time as a real possibility, these tax incentives are unfamiliar.

Income Taxes – The Marriage Bonus

Until 2013, partners in a same-sex union had to file separate tax returns designating each as single. If they had a dependent, one of them could qualify for "head of household" status.

In 2013, following <u>Windsor</u>, the IRS ruled that gay and lesbian couples had the option to submit a federal joint return instead.[17]

Couples who are married have the option to file taxes jointly as long as they are married by December 31st. One commentator notes that "Marriage bonuses can be as high as 20 percent of a couple's income and marriage penalties can be as high as 12 percent of a couple's income."[18] This is an option, not a requirement, and after marriage, spouses may file jointly or separately. While most couples prefer joint filing because it lowers taxes, separate filing is better for a minority of married couples.

Joint filing usually makes sense if both individuals are earning but one makes considerably more taxable income than the other. By combining incomes for filing, a married couple may be able to lower the overall tax bracket, because a spouse who does not earn

---

[17] Rev. Rule 2013-17
[18] www.taxfoundation.org/understanding-marriage-penalty-and-marriage-bonus

or who earns less than their partner may be able to pull the higher earning spouse into a lower bracket.

Another benefit of filing jointly is that certain deductions that would be unusable by one spouse can be harvested by the other. For instance, if one spouse has losses that exceed the amount he or she is able to claim in a given year under separate filing, filing jointly may enable those losses to be claimed in the current tax year rather than be lost or rolled forward.

Certain other tax benefits are only available to a married couple when they file jointly like the ability to make greater IRA contributions. In 2017, the maximum amount an individual can contribute to a traditional IRA is only $5,500 ($6,500.00 for those at least 50 years of age). If that individual has a non-working spouse, however, they may contribute the same amount to a Spousal IRA, doubling the amount of their pre-tax investments.

Married couples with charitable inclinations can also benefit from joint filing if their charitable contributions exceed the amount that an individual can deduct in a given year. Contributions to valid charitable organizations may be deducted up to 50 percent of the donor's adjusted gross income, and contributions to certain private foundations, veteran's organizations, fraternal societies, and cemetery organizations are limited to 30 percent adjusted gross income.[19] By filling jointly, married couples can double the amount of charitable contributions that they can deduct.

Another significant tax benefit of marriage involves the Home Sale Gain Exclusion, which allows a taxpayer to exclude up to $250,000 of gain from the sale of a principal residence if he or she has lived in it for at least two of the five years before the sale. That amount is doubled to $500,000 for married taxpayers who file a joint return. This increased exclusion is available to even a widowed spouse who remains unmarried and sells the couple's home within two years of their spouse's death.

Joint filing is also available to a qualifying widow or widower: an individual whose spouse has died, who has dependent children, and who remains unmarried may file jointly for two tax years following spouse's death, retaining the benefits of joint filing tax tables and the larger standard deduction.

Income Taxes – The Marriage Penalty

There are also a few possible downsides to filing jointly and even to marrying regardless of

---

[19] www.irs.gov/charities-non-profits/charitable-organizations/charitable-contribution-deductions

whether you file jointly or separately. A few dual-income couples incur a "marriage penalty" when filing income taxes: they owe more tax filing jointly than had they filed separately because their combined earnings push them into higher brackets. This can happen because the amount of income required for a married couple to fall into the four highest brackets – 25 percent, 28 percent, 33 percent, and 39.6 – are less than double the amount required for a single person. For example, "the 33 percent tax bracket for singles starts at $189,300 of taxable income but starts at $230,450 of taxable income (less that twice ($189,300) for married couples filing jointly."[20]

Table 1. 2016 Taxable Income Brackets and Rates (Estimate)

Rate	Single Filers	Married Joint Filers	Head of Household Filers
10%	$0 to $9,275	$0 to $18,550	$0 to 13,250
15%	$9,275 to $37,650	$18,550 to $75,300	$13,250 to $50,400
25%	$37,650 to $91,150	$75,300 to $151,900	$50,400 to 130,150
28%	$91,150 to $190,150	$151,900 to $231,450	$130,150 to $210,800
33%	$190,150 to $413,350	$231,450 to $413,350	$210,800 to $413,350
35%	$413,350 to $415,050	$413,350 to $466,950	$413,350 to $441,000
39.6%	$415,050+	$466,950+	$441,000+

*Source – The Tax Foundation

---

[20] www.taxfoundation.org/understanding-marriage-penalty-and-marriage-bonus

What's more, if a wealthy couple with high enough combined total income, may trigger the "Medicare surtax" by filing jointly, which amounts to 0.9% on earnings over $250,000. Couples who marry also increase their exposure to the Net Investment Income Tax (NIIT). As of Jan. 1, 2013, married couples filing jointly must pay a tax of 3.8% on net investment income above the threshold amount of $250,000 and married individual filing separately must pay 3.8% on income over $125,000. However, unmarried individuals do not pay the Net Investment Income Tax until their taxable income reaches $200,000.

Certain itemized deductions that have income thresholds may more difficult to obtain for joint filers. For instance, separate returns may help ensure a spouse with large medical bills can deduct those expenses. Medical expenses are deductible only once they rise to 10% of adjusted gross income or 7.5% if you or your spouse are 65 or older. If the spouse with medical bills files jointly with a spouse who has significant income, it is more difficult for the ailing spouse to reach that amount.

The marriage penalty also potentially affects lower earners, as combining both spouses' incomes could disqualify them from the Earned Income Tax Credit.

Joint filing can also mean that both spouses much either itemize deductions or claim the standard deduction: if one spouse itemizes deductions, so must the other, even if they have few itemized deductions and would be better off claiming the standard deduction.

Finally, and perhaps most crucially, joint filing means joint liability. A spouse who has concerns about claims their partner wants to make on a joint tax return should file separately. While there are certain exceptions for "innocent spouses" for tax claims made on a joint return, the general rule is that both spouses must sign and are jointly liable for errors or fraud on a joint return. This liability can mean that an innocent spouse can be held liable for both civil and criminal claims.

Estate Tax – the Marital Deduction

Estate taxes are a concern for few Americans today. Many states, including North Carolina, do not tax the transfer of assets at death, and very few estates are large enough to have to pay Federal taxes. Under Federal law, every individual has an exemption (the Applicable Exclusion Amount) of $5,490,000 in 2017 (indexed for inflation) from Estate or Gift taxes, meaning that they can give away up to $5,490,000 combined during life or at death.

Anything over that amount is taxed at roughly 40%.

Transfers to spouses (who are U.S. Citizens), however, are entirely exempt and do not count against the Applicable Exclusion Amount, meaning that assets given to a spouse during life or left to a spouse at death are not taxed at all, regardless of the amount.

There is also another estate tax benefit to marriage: "portability." If one spouse does not fully use their exemption through lifetime or testamentary gifts, the surviving spouse can add the remainder, the "Deceased Spouses Unused Exclusion Amount," to their own by filing an estate tax return. Thus, a married couple in 2017 has an effective Exclusion Amount of nearly $11,000,000.

In addition to these direct benefits, the marital deduction and portability also create a number of planning opportunities for those couples with estate tax exposure, providing immense estate tax planning benefits, often enabling married couples to reduce or eliminate estate tax exposure in ways that unmarried people cannot.

Marriage, Taxes and Attribution Rules

A lesser known but potentially profound implication of marriage on taxes arises from the fact that spouses are considered to own each other's assets for the purpose of applying certain rules under the Internal Revenue Code, for instance under §1563 or §267.

There are variations on "Family Attribution" rules throughout the Code, but take for example the one that applies to Partnership Taxation, found in Subchapter J.

IRC §704(e) was designed to prevent the intra-family assignment of income, sometimes used as a tax dodge by which a high earner will assign income to a lower taxed family member by labeling a family member as a partner and then allocating income to such family member. This provision stipulates that if three requirements are met, the arrangement will be voided.

There are three requirements for a partnership attribution between family members to avoid being disregarded. First, if capital is a significant income producing component of the business, then each family member must have an interest in the capital (not just an income interest). Second, the rate of return on donee's capital interest must not exceed rate of return on donor's capital interest. Third, the donor of the intra family interest must receive reasonable compensation for his or her services.

As with many of the questions raised by Obergefell, the precise details of how the courts will work this out are unresolved to date, but we can imagine some hypothetical situations. Take, for instance, a same sex couple who are also business partners in an LLC.

Their compensation arrangement may have been fine under §704 when they were separate, but might run afoul of family attribution rules after marriage. Indeed, for couples with significant assets or more complex planning, these family attribution rules found throughout the code can substantially affect the appropriateness of their current asset structure, potentially turning a tax or asset protection plan on its head.

The bottom line is that LGBT individuals with substantial assets need to carefully consider how marriage will impact their holdings.

Assets, Finances and Estate Planning

Beyond taxes, marriage impacts the assets and finances of spouses in a variety of ways. It confers survivorship rights to Social Security, Pension, or Qualified Retirement Plans, enables couples to hold property in a unique form called Tenancy by Entireties, gives a widowed spouse the right to an "Elective Share" of the deceased spouse's estate, and has many other effects. This section discusses some of those.

Social Security Income

Among the most obvious and most financially meaningful effects of marriage are Social Security spousal benefits, which are available to current spouses, widowed spouses or even ex-spouses.[21]

A spouse who has not worked enough to qualify for Social Security benefits may be able to receive their spouse's benefits if they are at least 62 years of age or are "any age and caring for a child entitled to receive benefits on [their] spouse's record who is younger than age 16 or disabled."[22]

Second, a spouse who is eligible for both their own retirement benefits and for benefits as a spouse can receive a combination of benefits equaling the higher spouses.[23] Alternately, they can claim a Social Security benefit based on their own earnings record or collect a spousal benefit that provides 50% of their spouse's Social Security benefit as calculated at full retirement age.

---

[21] www.thebalance.com/how-the-the-social-security-spouse-benefit-works-2388924
[22] www.faq.ssa.gov/link/portal/34011/34019/Article/3754/What-is-the-eligibility-for-Social-Security-spouse-s-benefits-and-my-own-retirement-benefits
[23] *Id.*

Individuals who are widowed before age 70 also have the right to choose between receiving their own or their deceased spouse's benefits. The surviving spouse can file for either their own benefit or as a widow(er), and then later switch if the numbers work favorably.

For instance, a widowed spouse might do this if their own benefit amount would be lower than their spouse's before age 70, but greater after, in which case they can claim the spouse's benefit until 70, and then switch to their own.

A person who is widowed after both they and their spouse have begun receiving Social Security benefits can continue to receive the larger of their benefit or their spouse's for the remainder of their lives, but not both. This may mean, however, that one whose spouse begins taking Social Security early, if they are widowed, will have reduced spousal benefits for the remainder of their life.[24]

Finally, and surprisingly to some people, marriage also confers the possibility that your spouse will be entitled to your Social Security benefits even after divorce in certain circumstances. Divorced spouses remain entitled to spousal benefits unless and until they remarry, and can receive a spousal benefit based on an ex-spouse's earnings history even if the ex-

---

[24] *Id.*

spouse has not yet filed for their own benefits, as long as the ex-spouse is 62 or older.[25]

Retirement Plan Benefits

Marriage has implications for retirement plans as well. For traditional pensions, 401(k) or other plans governed under ERISA, a surviving spouse is usually the automatic beneficiary of a retirement plan, has marital rights to plan benefits and often must consent in writing if the employee wishes to change a beneficiary.

Traditional Pensions

Traditional pensions, which are increasingly rare, are required by law to provide steady payments over the lifetime of the retiree and a surviving spouse, unless the beneficiary opts not to receive a spousal survivor benefit in favor of higher monthly payments during life. Making this election out of spousal coverage requires written consent from the spouse. The same restrictions apply to pension plans which give workers the option to take lump sum payments instead of annuity payments.

---

[25] www.thebalance.com/how-the-the-social-security-spouse-benefit-works-2388924

401(k)s

The impact of marriage on 401(k) savings can be immense. Married couples who both have 401(k)s at work can defer income tax on twice as much money as single people.

Moreover, couples who are not maxing out both of their 401(k) plans can decide whose has the better employer matching contributions. Better still is the possibility of receiving matches from both employers.

Spouses are also the default beneficiary of a 401(k) account balance upon the death of the account owner, and usually they must sign off on any alternative beneficiary. They have presumptive rights to these benefits under federal law, and they are subject to claims of equitable distribution under state law during divorce. The spouse's rights end there, however, as they have no ability to restrict the owner spouse's control of the account during marriage. Thus, they have no legal protections against poor investments, excessive spending or the account being rolled into an IRA, which does not require the spouse to be the beneficiary.

Individual Retirement Accounts

IRAs, by contrast with pensions and 401(k)s, are not governed by ERISA and do not have the same protections for spouses.[26]

For a spouse to be beneficiary of an IRA, they must be specifically named as a beneficiary on a beneficiary designation form. Marriage does significantly impact IRAs, however. Married couples can deduct IRA contributions up to higher income limits than individuals when they also have retirement accounts at work.

The tax deduction for traditional IRA contributions for married couples filing jointly, where the spouse making the IRA contribution is covered by a workplace retirement plan, phases out between $99,000 to $119,000, instead of $62,000 to $72,000 for individuals.

For an IRA contributor who is not covered by a workplace retirement plan and is married to

---

[26] This is true even if a 401(k) is rolled into an IRA. In a recent case, Charles Schwab v. Debickero (U.S. Ct. App., 9th Cir., No. 07-15261, Jan. 22, 2010) a husband rolled his 401(k) into an IRA with Charles Schwab & Company after he retired. He named his children as the IRA's beneficiaries. After he died, his wife claimed that she was entitled to the account funds as his surviving spouse. She argued that because her husband rolled his 401(k) into the IRA, she should receive the same protections that the 401(k) gave her. The court disagreed, finding that the IRAs are excluded from ERISA coverage even if the funds originated in a 401(k).

someone who is covered, the deduction is phased out if the couple's income is between $186,000 and $196,000. For a married individual filing a separate return who is covered by a workplace retirement plan, the phase-out range is $0 to $10,000.

Spouses also have additional options when it comes to rolling over an inherited IRA: they may treat it as their own and roll it into their own retirement account or keep it as a separate IRA and taking required minimum distributions based upon the deceased spouse's required minimum distribution schedule. This option means that a spouse may elect to defer income from an inherited IRA longer than a non-spouse beneficiary, enhancing the benefits of tax deferred growth in that IRA.

Estate Planning

Because the legal protections that marriage affords spouses extend to incapacity and death, estate planning for married couples is very different than estate planning for individuals.

Real Property

Married couples also enjoy the right to hold property as Tenants by the Entireties during life, a form of legal ownership only available to married couples that confers survivorship rights on the widowed spouse. In North Carolina, only real property – land or houses – can be owned in Tenancy by the Entireties. While both spouses remain alive, Tenancy by the Entireties property is protected from the creditors of individual spouses (except for federal tax liens). At death, Tenancy by Entireties property passes directly to the other spouse, avoiding probate. In North Carolina, if property deeded to two married people, there is a presumption that it is held Tenancy by the Entireties.

In addition, North Carolina law allows an individual to exempt up to $35,000 in equity in real estate from creditors, including bankruptcy.[27] This homestead property is $60,000 for married couples. You may also exempt "alimony, support, separate maintenance, and child support payments or funds that have been received or to which the debtor is entitled, to the extent the payments or funds are reasonably necessary for the support of the debtor or any dependent of the debtor."[28]

Health Care Decisions for Married People

Spouses have legal obligations to each other and enjoy corresponding presumptive rights to take care for each other. Before <u>Obergefell,</u> LGBT individuals commonly faced problems with

---

[27] N.C.G.S. § 1C-1601(a)
[28] *Id.*

visitation or health care decision making for their partners. Marital status directly affects these rights, and while it is advisable for everyone to have a Health Care Power of Attorney and a Living Will to set forth their wishes for end of life care and avoid the application of legal defaults described below, it is especially imperative for unmarried LGBT couples, whose have no statutory right to make healthcare decisions for their partners.

N.C.G.S. § 90-21.13(c) provides a framework for "consent to medical treatment on behalf of a patient who is comatose or otherwise lacks capacity to make or communicate health care decisions." The law provides the following order of preference for making these decisions: an individual named in a health care power of attorney (if not revoked by court order); a guardian; a health care attorney in fact appointed by statute; a spouse; a majority of children; a majority of siblings; and finally "[a]n individual who has an established relationship with the patient, who is acting in good faith on behalf of the patient, and who can reliably convey the patient's wishes."[29]

Obviously marriage affects this order of succession directly, as spouses are able to decide if there is no guardian or health care attorney-in-fact. In this case, an unmarried LGBT individual

---

[29] N.C.G.S. 90-21.13(c)(7)

whose partner is ailing faces the very real prospect of being passed over for a child or sibling in making deathbed decisions. In addition to the direct inclusion of spouses in the statute cited above, there is also a judicial tendency to favor a spouse when appointing a guardian in the event of a contested hearing.[30]

Probate

Surviving spouses also enjoy preferential treatments under entitled North Carolina's Probate Code and Elective Share statutes. Section 28A-28-4 (1) of the North Carolina General Statutes provides that a surviving spouse to be appointed Personal Representative of a decedent's estate unless "the clerk of superior court in the discretion of the clerk of superior court determines that the best interests of the estate otherwise require." As Personal Representative, the spouse is then responsible for the process of probating the estate and is not required to depend or wait on a third party.

In addition, where a surviving spouse is the sole beneficiary of an estate, N.C.G.S. § 28A-28 entitles them to "summary administration." The surviving spouse may file a petition for summary administration with the clerk of superior court of the county where the decedent was domiciled at

---

[30] www.ksquaredlegal.com/wp-content/uploads/2015/06/Guardianship-Introduction-Packet.pdf

the time of death. If granted, this procedure allows the spouse an expedited process to assume the assets and liabilities of the deceased spouse. Summary administration is not available if the decedent's will provides that it is not available or if the devise to the surviving spouse is in trust.

The right of a widowed spouse to an "elective share" of the deceased spouse's estate is perhaps the most financially significant impact of marriage under state probate law. N.C.G.S. § 30-3.1 provides that "[t]he surviving spouse of a decedent who dies domiciled in this State has a right to claim an 'elective share', which means an amount equal to (i) the applicable share of the Total Net Assets [...] as follows:

1) If the surviving spouse was married to the decedent for less than five years, fifteen percent (15%) of the Total Net Assets.
2) If the surviving spouse was married to the decedent for at least five years but less than 10 years, twenty-five percent (25%) of the Total Net Assets.
3) If the surviving spouse was married to the decedent for at least 10 years but less than 15 years, thirty-three percent (33%) of the Total Net Assets.
4) If the surviving spouse was married to the decedent for 15 years or more, fifty percent (50%) of the Total Net Assets."

The statute is drafted very broadly, extending even to assets like life insurance benefits and retirement plan benefits that are otherwise asset protected. These elective share rights mean that it is normally impossible to disinherit a spouse in North Carolina without a valid pre or post-nuptial agreement. A spouse who is not left the statutory minimum and is not bound by a pre or post-nuptial agreement may file an action in court to enforce their elective share rights, potentially profoundly affecting the division of all of all assets the decedent owned at their death.

Finally, a surviving spouse has rights regarding real estate owned by their deceased spouse. The surviving spouse may either elect to take a life estate – a right to use of the property for their remaining life – in one-third of the deceased spouse's real estate, or, instead, may elect a life estate in their current home if it was owned by the decedent at the time of death.

Wills and Trusts

Estate planning with wills or trusts may also be different for married people. A will is a legal document by which a person provides for the transfer of assets at death.

Wills are governed by North Carolina law, which provides detailed description of what is required both to make and to carry out, or probate, a will.

A Revocable Living Trust is an alternative to a will used by estate planning attorneys to help clients (1) protect assets for beneficiaries, (2) avoid probate and (3) plan for incapacity. Trusts are a type of legal entity that vary enormously in nature and purpose, and a full discussion of trusts is far beyond the scope of this guide. We will discuss only revocable living trusts used for estate planning and a few derivatives of these.

A trust is a legal entity that can own and dispose of assets. As with a company, which has shareholders, a board of directors and officers, the trust divides up ownership of those assets into different roles. An individual or couple, the Grantor(s), creates a trust by signing the proper documentation, and then contribute assets to it. The trust gives responsibility and ownership of those assets to a named individual, the Trustee. The trustee is charged with holding and distributing the assets for the benefit of a third party, the Beneficiary or Beneficiaries, per the terms in the Trust.

With a normal revocable living trust, during the life of the Grantor, he or she may revoke or change it at any time, may serve as their own trustee, and may remain the Beneficiary. As a result, there are no practical implications for taxes or for asset protection until either the incapacity or death of one or more Grantors. At that point, the trust becomes irrevocable and "changes shape" to accommodate the new circumstances. During incapacity, the trust assets are used for the incapacitated Grantor's needs, and at death they are distributed to the beneficiaries according to its terms.

What all this means for those considering estate planning, and in particular for an LGBT couple considering marriage, is that marriage dramatically affects how a will or a revocable living trust should be structured. Trusts may be joint or separate, a joint trust may hold "separate property," may include special provisions intended to qualify assets for the marital deductions discussed above (a Qualified Terminal Interest Property or QTIP Trust), can help avoid probate, but remain subject to elective share rights.

The availability or appropriateness of other, irrevocable trusts that serve more nuanced estate tax or asset protection purposes, such as a Spousal Limited Access Trust (SLAT) or a Qualified Personal Residence Trust (QPRT) depend upon marital status as well.

LGBT individuals considering marriage should take care to evaluate how it will affect their financial and estate planning, and if necessary contact an appropriate professional to help in this assessment.

Chapter 3: Action Items

Aside from understanding the benefits that marriage affords to all LGBT individuals going forward, there are a few areas where LGBT individuals may still be able to take steps to retroactively assert the rights that Obergefell has established.

As stated above, precisely what Obergefell means for LGBT rights in a variety of areas remains to be determined by the courts. One commentator notes that the effects the decision "will cascade into virtually every legal venue, from tax to contracts, from bankruptcy to divorce, and from parentage issues to spousal immunity concerns in criminal law. [...] There currently are, and will continue to be, complicated lawsuits concerning the potential retroactive vestment of marital property rights for same-sex married couples, which may also impact third parties such as purchasers, mortgagees, and title insurers."[31]

Practically speaking, this means that the discussion of some of the possible opportunities for LGBT couples going forward is tentative, subject to change, and provided here only as items for consideration.

---

[31] Lee-ford Tritt, Moving Forward by Looking Back: The Retroactive Application of Obergefell, Wisconsin Law Review, Vol. 5, p. 873, 2016.

Whether any such opportunity is available for a given person or couple is a fact specific and legally tricky enquiry, and anyone pursuing such claims needs the help of appropriate counsel.

Retroactive Claims

Individuals who were part of a civil union, a domestic partnership or a legal marriage before Obergefell, and who were wrongly denied marital rights under state or federal law may have the opportunity to seek redress. Such individuals may be able to take retroactive measures such as filing amended tax returns or seeking back payment of spousal pension or veteran's benefits.

Federal Income Tax Refunds

First, there are likely few possible claims for federal income tax refunds at this point, as the IRS announced that it would recognize the validity of all marriages for federal tax purposes in Revenue Ruling 2013-17 after the Windsor decision. The normal statutory period within which one can amend a return under IRC section 6511 the later of three years from the time it was filed or two years from the time it was paid.

To amend Federal tax returns under, you must file a form 1040x and show the IRS the amount of the overpayment and a form 843 Claim for Refund and Request for Abatement. You must show clearly the legal grounds for the overpayment. If it is not possible to file these forms in a timely fashion, one may be able to toll the statute of limitations by filing an "informal" Claim for Refund, a letter to the IRS stating that you are seeking a refund for a specific reason.

When considering making refunds, however, it is important to be careful. In some cases, it is possible that you could have increased tax liability. Filing and amended return may also make you a heightened target for an audit, carries with it the same liabilities for misreporting that apply to all filings, and also has the additional risk of sanction under IRC §6676, which imposes a 20% penalty on amounts deemed excessive.

North Carolina State Income Tax Refunds

In 2017, LGBT couples are more likely to have refunds available to them under state law, as North Carolina is one of the states that did not permit any form of gay marriage until Obergefell. The statute of limitations for filing an amended return in North Carolina is the same as under federal law, meaning that LGBT couples who were married before <u>Obergefell</u>, for instance under the laws of another state, and subsequently denied the right to file jointly under North Carolina law, may be still able to file refunds.

To make changes, North Carolina taxpayers will need to file Form D-400 with the Department of Revenue. You must fill in the circle on Form D-400 indicating Amended Return, complete and attach Form D-400 Schedule AM, 2015 North Carolina Amended Schedule, to the front of Form D-400 and attach all required schedules and supporting forms.

Given the extent to which many of the specific questions <u>Obergefell</u> raised involving the details of equality are still unresolved by the courts, individuals whose claims to a refund depend upon the resolution of pending cases should consider filing a "protective claim." If the time limit for amending a return is getting close but there is ongoing litigation (for example, you are involved in estate litigation that could affect tax liability) or some other contingency that may affect your taxes, you can file for a protective claim to preserve the right to recover the specified amount after the even if the contingency has only been resolved after the statute of limitations has passed.

To do so, the taxpayer must file Form 843 with the IRS specifying the grounds for the protective claim.[32]

Federal Estate Tax Refunds

It is possible that litigation in the wake of Obergefell will enable LGBT individuals to amend estate tax returns beyond the normal statute of limitations. Lawsuits seeking to define the precise parameters of Obergefell's retroactivity may assert Constitutional claims that the laws prohibiting gay people from marrying and filing jointly were *void ab initio*, invalid from their codification.

While such suits are pending, LGBT individuals who may be entitled to estate tax refunds based upon such claims (for instance if they paid estate taxes on the death of a spouse prior to Obergefell and were wrongly denied a marital deduction) and who wishes to avoid the statute of limitations expiring, should file a "protective claim" under state or federal law.

The process for amending an estate tax return, which is described in IRS Revenue Procedure 2011-48, is a little different.[33] First, the estate must file a separate protective claim for refund for each potential estate claim or expense before

---

[32] See Nucorp, Inc. v. United States, 23 Cl. Ct. 234 (1991)
[33] www.irs.gov/irb/2011-42_IRB/ar13.html

the IRC Section 6511 filing deadline. The protective claim may be filed on Schedule PC of the federal estate tax return (expected to debut on the 2012 Form 706) or on a separate Form 843 (Claim for Refund and Request for Abatement). Each filing must satisfy numerous requirements regarding content set forth in the revenue procedure, including a written statement, under penalty of perjury, of each ground upon which a refund is claimed; an explanation of why payment of the underlying claim or expense is delayed; reference to other related deductions already taken and other protective claims previously made; and evidence of the claimant's authority to act on behalf of the estate or the decedent.

Next, the estate must make sure that the IRS receives and accepts the protective claim. The IRS may reject a claim that is defective in form or substance. Otherwise, the IRS will notify the estate in writing that the protective claim has been received. The revenue procedure advises the estate to contact the IRS if the estate has not received notice of receipt from the IRS within 60 to 180 days (depending on the form of the filing).

The third step is to wait until the contingency is resolved. Within 90 days after the underlying claim or expense is paid or the amount at issue becomes certain and no longer subject to contingency (whichever is later), the estate must notify the IRS that it wants a particular claim for refund to be considered and ruled upon. The revenue procedure provides requirements for content similar to those for the initial filing. The refund ultimately arising from each claim will be determined by considering the effect of the claim on the marital and charitable deductions.

Protective Claims and North Carolina Taxes

In North Carolina, the Department of Revenue will accept a protective claim for refund provided it (1) is filed before the expiration of the statutory refund claim period; (2) identifies and describes the contingencies affecting the claim; (3) is sufficiently clear and definite to alert the Department of Revenue as to the essential nature of the claim; and (4) identifies the tax schedule and the specific year for which the protective claim is filed. There is no special form for filing a protective claim. The North Carolina Department of Revenue will accept any written submission provided it contains all the required elements.[34]

Filing a protective claim is an option for couples trying to make constitutional claims for refunds so that they can preserve the right to amend their returns until their constitutional claim is adjudicated. For example, a couple entered a

---

[34] N.C. Gen. Stat. § 105-241.6(b)(5); www.dor.state.nc.us/taxes/individual/protective.html

domestic partnership because were refused a license to marry and therefore could not claim an estate tax marital deduction at the death of one partner may want to pursue a constitutional claim that would enable them to seek redress despite the statute of limitations having passed.

They may want to file a protective claim to ensure that they can obtain amend their return once the constitutional claim is resolved.[35]

While the tax implications of marriage are discussed more fully above, it is helpful to recall here the types of tax benefits that marriage confers when considering possible constitutional claims or amended returns. LGBT couples may have missed out on things like the marital deduction, use of capital losses, adoption benefits, special exclusions for spousal gift and estate taxes, exclusion of employer provided medical care for a spouse, or the use of portability of a spouse's unused exclusion amount.[36]

---

[35] www.blog.aicpa.org/2013/09/irs-guidance-following-doma-decision.html#sthash.eUtiMYop.dpbs

[36] On the question of amending an estate tax return for spousal portability, see *Windsor* and more specifically Rev. Rul. 2013-17 (applicable as of Sept. 16, 2013), in which the IRS treats same sex couples as being married and states can file an amended returns or claim for refunds if the three year statutory period has not expired. This seems to say that for couples who were legally married in one state but lived in another not recognizing the marriage who had one spouse die with no ability for a spousal exclusion because it is prior to this revenue ruling, now the

ERISA, Employee, Veterans, Health Benefits

Widowed spouses may be able to file retroactively for benefits or appeal a prior denial of benefits under a retirement plan if they were previously disallowed for reasons that violate Obergefell.

While some such claims will fall because of the broad "abuse of discretion" standard courts apply to plan administrators, in some instances LGBT individuals denied benefits will have legitimate claims.

IRS Revenue Ruling 2013-17 allowed for on the retroactive application of the federal recognition of same sex marriages to certain federal employee benefits. Under that ruling, qualified plans have to recognize same sex spouses as spouses for purposes of inheritance and rollover rights as of September 16, 2013. Same sex couples can apply this ruling retroactively to employer-provided health care coverage or fringe benefits that may have previously resulted in a tax overpayment by the now recognized spouse.

---

surviving spouse may could amend the return to elect portability (if in the statutory time frame) to be able to use the deceased spouse's unused exclusion.

Defined benefit and defined contribution plans also have marital provisions, and if a same sex spouse was denied the benefits of those provisions before or after Obergefell, they may have a claim. For example, some plans use a Qualified Joint and Survivor Annuity payment (usually in defined benefit plans), meaning that payments made on the death of a first spouse should have been made on the death of the second.[37]

LGBT individuals who were previously denied healthcare benefits that, according to Obergefell, should have extended to them, may be able to appeal those denials or make claims for refund. Going forward, as well, spouses may be able to receive more favorable health care coverage under spousal provisions, and may be able to use tax favored healthcare accounts such as HSA, FSA, and HRA.

---

[37] www.irs.gov/retirement-plans/plan-participant-employee/retirement-topics-qualified-joint-and-survivor-annuity

Conclusion

We hope that you have found this guide helpful. The good news is that, in the wake of <u>Obergefell</u>, LGBT couples now enjoy the same marital rights as straight couples. The bad news is that (1) many claims for retroactive remedies will be barred by statutes of limitations, (2) the exact extent of remedies available as a result of <u>Obergefell</u> is unclear at this point and (3) the progress of which <u>Obergefell</u> was a seminal moment is neither complete nor secure.

Much has and will be written about <u>Obergefell</u>, in praise and condemnation, and as this is simply a legal guide, suffice it to say that <u>Obergefell</u> is the case that LGBT advocates have long dreamed of – sweeping both in its rhetoric and its effect. Though the precise details of how this broad mandate will interact with a variety of state and federal constitutional, statutory and regulatory provisions must be parsed, the bottom line is that state actors are prohibited from discriminating against same-sex couples in marriage and must extend them the rights afforded heterosexual married couples.

Many LGBT individuals and allies have expressed concern that the Trump Administration may roll back progress on marriage equality, or that the appointment of a conservative judge to the Supreme Court may even lead to <u>Obergefell</u>'s overturning. It is impossible to know what will happen, but the judicial doctrine of *stare decisis*, which encourages judges to view prior decisions with an added measure of deference, combined with the growing national majority in favor of marriage equality, should make it difficult for this progress to be truly reversed. It may be, or rather I should say, may it be, that Justice Kennedy's words on gay marriage are among the last we hear from the Court:

"No union is more profound than marriage, for it embodies the highest ideals of love, fidelity, devotion, sacrifice, and family. In forming a marital union, two people become something greater than once they were. As some of the petitioners in these cases demonstrate, marriage embodies a love that may endure even past death. It would misunderstand these men and women to say they disrespect the idea of marriage. Their plea is that they do respect it, respect it so deeply that they seek to find its fulfillment for themselves. Their hope is not to be condemned to live in loneliness, excluded from one of civilization's oldest institutions. They ask for equal dignity in the eyes of the law. The Constitution grants them that right."[38]

---

[38] Obergefell v. Hodges, 135 S. Ct. 2071 (2015).

About the Author

Lorin graduated with high honors from the University of Alabama School of Law. During law school, he served on the Campbell Moot Court Board, the Journal of the Legal Profession, and was a Hugo Black Scholar. Prior to that, he concentrated in English and Philosophy at the Florida Atlantic University Honors College. In August of 2016, Lorin completed his Master's degree in Taxation (LLM) at the University of Florida's Graduate Studies Program, gaining an in depth understanding of the legal intricacies of individual, estate and business tax.

Lorin focuses his practice in estate planning, business and tax law, consulting with clients on matters from simple wills to drafting irrevocable trusts to address complex estate planning needs. He also works closely with business owners on issues from establishing or selling businesses to integrating business succession and estate planning to the use of advanced planning trusts to minimize tax exposure.

Since law school, Lorin has worked as a volunteer lawyer representing criminal defendants and civil plaintiffs. He has helped juvenile defendants navigate the criminal justice process and researched matters of both state and federal criminal law.

He is a member of the North Carolina State Bar, the 28th District Bar Association, the Young Lawyer's Division, and serves on several local non-profit boards and committees.

Lorin can be reached at 1-828-696-1811 or lorin@strausslaw.com.

www.ingramcontent.com/pod-product-compliance
Lightning Source LLC
Chambersburg PA
CBHW050017230526
45470CB00003B/1003